Myths and Legends Kit

Jon Mayhew

Illustrated by **Joe Todd-Stanton**

OXFORD
UNIVERSITY PRESS

Contents

Welcome, Storytellers!

What makes a myth? How is it different from a legend? If you were going to make up your own myth or legend, how would you do it? In this book I'm going to share the secrets of the best myths and legends from around the world and challenge you to write one of your own.

We're going to scatter their main ingredients all over the floor, pick them up and create something new. By the end of this book, you should be a master maker of myths or a leader in laying down legends!

So what *are* myths, and how are they different from legends?

MYTHS:

- give us a fictional explanation for a **natural phenomenon** (for example, why elephants have trunks)
- try to explain the world and its mysteries
- are used by many cultures to pass on cultural, religious or spiritual beliefs.

LEGENDS:

- are more likely to be about real people, places or even objects
- may be based on something that did exist or happen in the past but which has been exaggerated or changed
- tell us about the way particular people lived and what they believed
- often deal with issues that are still important to us today, for example being brave or a good leader.

BOTH MYTHS AND LEGENDS:

- are set in a distant past or in the early history of a culture
- are traditional stories
- are passed down from generation to generation
- may contain gods.

Guess what? You're going to use these ingredients to cook up your own myth or legend. As you read the retellings in this book, look out for the symbols that represent each ingredient.

INGREDIENTS FOR A MYTH OR LEGEND

1 Hero or heroine

2 Villain, threat or problem

3 Monster or creature

4 Unintended consequence

5 Quest, mission or great deed

6 Set a long time ago, in a distant land or far-off realm

7 Gods and enchantment

8 Enchanted objects or weapons

9 Explanation

World Map of Myths and Legends

The Ancient Greeks told stories, the Aztecs told stories, there are myths and legends from Africa, India, America – all over the world – and they have to start somewhere! Use this map to keep track of where the myths and legends in this book come from.

GREENLAND

Why is the Raven Black?

BRITAIN

CANADA

USA

Set

Tsonokwa, Ch'eni

Alligators in the Sewers

N

W

S

Introduction to Myths and Legends

Passing the story on

Myths and legends are both types of story, and a long time ago they were told rather than written in books. Most people couldn't read, and some cultures didn't write things down but passed their myths and legends orally from parent to child, grandparent to grandchild. While one storyteller may have memorized a story word for word, some people might remember it differently and change it slightly. They might even change it depending on who they are telling it to.

Let's look at how one story can become another ...

The Tsonokwa

The story of the Tsonokwa (*say* ta-son-ak-wa) comes from the mythology of the Kwakwaka'wakw tribe in Canada. The Tsonokwa were blood-sucking, cannibal giants (usually female) who lived in the forest, preying on hunters or children who strayed too far into the deep woods.

Here's the basic myth:

A <u>Tsonokwa</u> ③ **terrorizes** the land, <u>devouring animals and people</u> ② . The giantess drinks the blood of her victims. Finally, <u>a brave warrior</u> ① <u>decides to kill the monster</u> ⑥ . The warrior lies down in the forest where the Tsonokwa lives and pretends to be dead. The giantess sees the warrior lying there and thinks, "I'll take him back to my camp and roast him on my fire!"

But when the Tsonokwa gets back to camp, the warrior springs to life and <u>pushes the giantess into her own fire</u> ⑤ . The Tsonokwa burns to the finest ash. Each tiny fragment of ash <u>turns into a miniature version of the big monster</u> ④ and flies out into the world to suck the blood of every human in the land.

<u>And that is how mosquitoes are created</u> ⑨ .

Other tribes in North America called the Tsonokwa 'Sasquatch' (*say* sass-kwotch), but it was essentially the same monster and the same stories were told about them. So imagine: that tale is told, but the next person who tells it can't remember it exactly and they change something. There's no knowing how many times that might happen before it becomes a different tale altogether.

Now turn the page to read the same story which has been changed for a different audience ...

If you were to tell the Tsonokwa myth to an audience of children, you may want them to pick up on a different meaning. Just think, these stories were told long ago by people who lived close to nature and were aware of how dangerous their environment was. Wild animals such as bears and wolves roamed close by, and it would be easy to get lost in deep, dark forests.

This tale was told by the Lummi tribe from the same area. Can you see that it is very nearly the same, but gives an explanation for a different natural phenomenon?

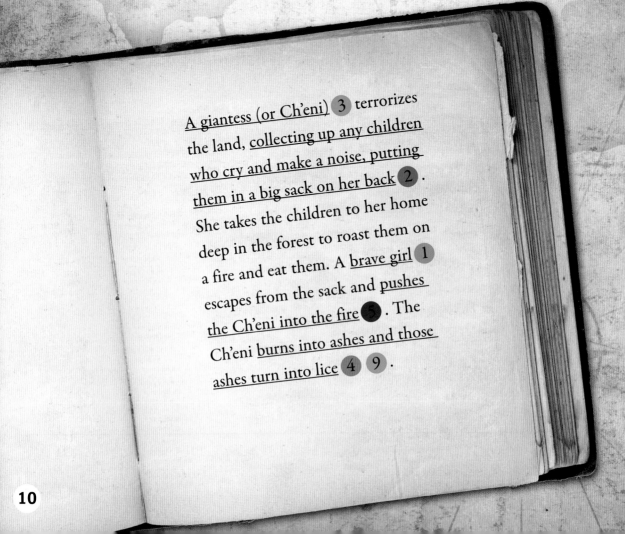

A giantess (or Ch'eni) ③ terrorizes the land, collecting up any children who cry and make a noise, putting them in a big sack on her back ② . She takes the children to her home deep in the forest to roast them on a fire and eat them. A brave girl ① escapes from the sack and pushes the Ch'eni into the fire ⑤ . The Ch'eni burns into ashes and those ashes turn into lice ④ ⑨ .

Perhaps the story is told this way to warn children about the dangers of being noisy in the forest. Making noise or sounds of distress could attract predators and put them in peril.

Perhaps the Lummi tribe were bothered by a different type of pest from the one affecting the Kwakwaka'wakw tribe. That's why one story explains where mosquitoes came from, and the other story is about why there are lice.

The Amazing Travelling Tale

When people from different cultures meet, they might swap their traditional tales. The north-western coast of Canada isn't too far from Russia. It's possible that Native American tribes and people from Russia traded with each other and swapped stories. The European story *Hansel and Gretel* includes a witch being pushed into an oven as well. Early European settlers could have brought the story over and told it to the Lummi people.

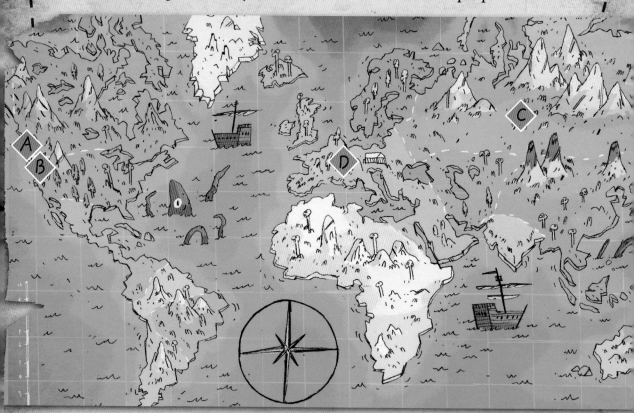

Perhaps you have heard of the Russian tale, *Baba Yaga*? Although this story isn't strictly a myth or legend, it has lots in common with the Tsonokwa myth and *Hansel and Gretel*. Why not look it up and check its ingredients out for yourself? Maybe the story of Hansel and Gretel was inspired by the tale of Baba Yaga.

	Kwakwaka'wakw tribe, Canada A	Lummi tribe, North America/ Canadian borders B	Russia C	Germany, Europe D
Story name/plot	Tsonokwa	Ch'eni	Baba Yaga	Hansel and Gretel
Female monster/ witch eager to eat children	✓	✓	✓	✓
Dwells in forests	✓	✓	✓	✓
Hero escapes	✓	✓	✓	✓
Monster/witch meets sticky end	✓	✓	✓	✓

Now we know that stories change when different people tell them. And as myths and legends are stories, too, it is probably all right for you to make up your own!

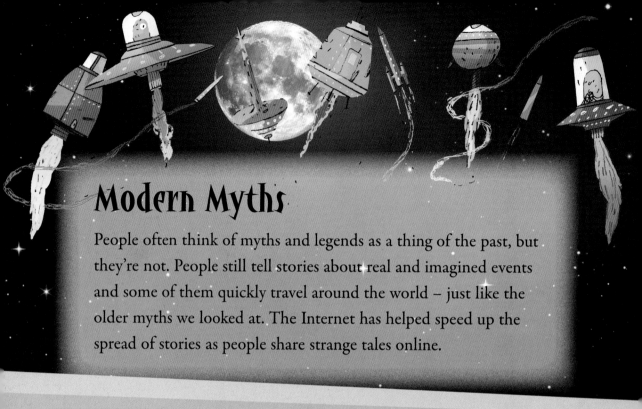

Modern Myths

People often think of myths and legends as a thing of the past, but they're not. People still tell stories about real and imagined events and some of them quickly travel around the world – just like the older myths we looked at. The Internet has helped speed up the spread of stories as people share strange tales online.

Alligators in the sewer

One **urban legend** says that in the 1930s many people from New York brought baby alligators home from their holidays in Florida. As the alligators grew, their owners realized that having a two-and-a-half-metre-long carnivorous reptile in the house wasn't sensible. They flushed them down the drain. Now people will tell you that they know someone who has seen huge reptiles in the sewers.

Other modern myths include secret government departments that deal with unusual incidents. You may have seen the *Men in Black* movies, but the modern myth came first. People who claim to have seen aliens from outer space often describe being approached by mysterious men dressed in black suits. Sometimes these men in black are human and other times they seem distinctly alien, but they always warn the person to keep quiet about what they have witnessed.

Why not write your own modern myth? It could give a warning, describe how something strange happened or talk about a mysterious event from not long ago. Just remember: it must be believable!

Ingredients for a modern myth

- It can be scary or give a warning. These tales aren't like the stories of the past that try to explain something.

- The teller will not usually have experienced the event themselves. The person in the myth will be 'a friend of a friend' or 'a girl I used to live next door to'.

- The story should be realistic enough to convince your audience that it really happened.

Myths

How it all happened

One feature of myths is that they can be used to pass on religious or spiritual beliefs, as they try to answer bigger questions that we ask, such as "Where are we from?" or "How did the world come to exist?"

Often in these stories, powerful gods or giants fight and make geographical features such as valleys and mountains. They might cry and create great oceans of salt tears, or they send down animals to **colonize** the sea and land. The following story demonstrates how powerful and tricky the gods can be.

Eos and Tithonus

This tale from Ancient Greece is a simple myth that explains where grasshoppers come from.

Eos <u>1</u> was a **Titan** and a <u>goddess</u> 7 of the dawn. Every morning, she would rise from her home <u>at the ocean's edge</u> 6 , bringing the promise of a new day.

Eos was very beautiful and she fell in love with a handsome young man called <u>Tithonus</u> 1 .

But <u>Tithonus was **mortal** and would die, whereas Eos would live forever</u> 2 . She couldn't bear to think of life without Tithonus.

So Eos approached Zeus, <u>chief of all the gods, and asked him to make Tithonus **immortal** 7</u>. Zeus agreed and Eos returned to her true love.

They lived happily for many years but then one day, Eos noticed a thread of silver in Tithonus's hair. A little later, wrinkles appeared around his eyes. <u>Tithonus was ageing 4</u>.

As the years became decades, Tithonus became more and more frail. His legs failed him and he lost his eyesight. Eventually, Tithonus lost his mind and the ability to speak properly.

Eos went back to Zeus to ask why he had not granted her wish.
"I did," said Zeus. "But you forgot to ask for the gift of **eternal youth**."

And so, Tithonus grew older and older until he was just a scrap of skin and bone.

Unable to bear his suffering any more, <u>Eos turned him into a grasshopper 7</u> and set him free. <u>And that is where grasshoppers come from 9</u>.

Same Question, Different Story

Here are two myths to explain another natural phenomenon – why the sea is salty.

The first myth is from the United Kingdom.

Two brothers lived long ago ⑥. One was very rich and <u>the other was terribly poor</u> ①. The poor brother found <u>an enchanted hand mill</u> ⑧, and whatever he wished for came out of the mill when he turned its handle. However, it would not stop turning until he said the word 'enough'.

The poor brother now lived a happy and comfortable life but <u>his rich brother became jealous</u> ②. He asked to borrow the hand mill and took it out to sea on his fishing boat. He caught a huge load of fish and promptly wished the mill to provide him with salt to preserve his catch. The mill began grinding out salt but the brother could not remember what he needed to say to make it stop. He tried everything he could think of, but <u>the boat filled with salt and sank</u> ④. <u>And there it lies today, still grinding salt into the sea</u> ⑨.

The second myth is from the Philippines. It was told to me by author Candy Gourlay and explains the same thing in a different way.

Once, a <u>friendly giant</u> ① named Ang-ngalo fell in love with Sipnget, <u>goddess of the dark</u> 7 . She <u>demanded he build a palace for her in the middle of the ocean</u> ② . As she was tired of the dark, Sipnget wanted her palace to be made of shining white bricks.

Now, Ang-ngalo was a tunnelling and building giant and so he made Sipnget bricks of the purest white salt. With them, he made bridges that <u>spanned the waters</u> ⑤ and called many thousands of builders to help him. They worked day and night but their noise woke <u>the Ocean</u> ② , who grew angry at being disturbed. The waters rose and <u>washed the men and salt bricks away</u> ④ . <u>And that is why the sea is salty</u> 9 .

With a partner, decide on a theme that explains where something in the natural world comes from. Now each write your myth about it without comparing notes. See how different their version is from yours!

Mix Your Own Myth

You're nearly ready to make up your own myth! Here are my top tips:

1. **Start at the end! What does your myth explain?**

You could describe where a particular creature came from. You might think of how geological features such as volcanoes, rivers or mountains came to exist. It could be something smaller such as "Why do dogs bark?" or "Why do skunks smell?"

2. **Choose your characters**

Who are your characters going to be? Heroes? Gods? Animals? Characters are always larger than life. They get angry easily and take their revenge, or they are too good to be true. They are *never* average!

3. **What's your problem?**

What is making the characters unhappy?

4. **What's your solution?**

How are your characters going to make themselves (or someone else) happy? What action do they take?

5. **And that is why ...**

It's good if you can end your myth with something like, "And that is why ... " because it summarizes the whole point of the myth.

Plan your story

In the chart below, I've started to work out the structure of a myth. I've also shown how a traditional Inuit myth fits this plan to get you started.

Hint: Myths always happened a long time ago!

Time and Location: When and where is it happening?	Long ago, in the North Pole ...
The Problem: Is a monster destroying things? Is a creature unhappy?	None of the creatures had any colour.
Action: Does someone say or do something wrong? Does one of the characters wish or ask for something?	Raven painted Snow Goose white with little black under-feathers. Snow Goose did the same for Raven. Raven said he didn't want to be the same as Snow Goose.
Reaction: The unforeseen consequence!	Snow Goose became angry and emptied the pot of black paint all over Raven ...
Explanation: The end of the story.	And that is why Ravens are black.

Did you find all of these ingredients in the Raven story? 6 2 4 9

Now it's over to you! Copy the chart and use it to plan out your own myth.

Legends
A legendary figure

First, have a look back at the definition on pages 4–5 to remind yourself what the features of a legend are.

A good example of a legendary figure is Alexander the Great. Alexander ruled the Ancient Greek kingdom of Macedon between 356 and 323 BCE. He conquered many lands and created an empire which included countries that are now modern-day Greece, Turkey, Pakistan, Iran, Iraq and Egypt. Stories about him began to spring up in all the countries he conquered.

The Gordian knot

Alexander the Great's **1** armies had pushed south-east into what we now know as Turkey. The men had fought hard and they were exhausted **2**. Alexander needed a sign to show his men that they couldn't be defeated as long as they followed him.

Alexander's advisors told him about the city of Gordium, the ancient capital of the country of Phrygia. Phrygia was once ruled by King Midas who, a century before, had left an ox cart tied to a stake outside the temple of Zeus. It was said that he who untied the knot that fastened the cart to the stake would become King of Phrygia **5** and defeat the Persians. Many had tried and failed. Alexander took his army to try to untie the knot.

Alexander asked his advisors if it mattered how the complex knot was untied. When they said it didn't, he drew his sword and cut straight through it! The knot unravelled and Alexander declared himself ruler of Phrygia. That night there was a violent thunderstorm, which people said proved Zeus 7 approved of Alexander claiming his rightful place as ruler.

The legend lives on …

The legend of the Gordian knot is still used today as an example of how to find a simple, and sometimes **drastic**, solution to a complex problem. The term used to describe this is the 'Alexandrian solution'.

It is possible that some elements of this legend are true, but the main purpose of the legend is to show that Alexander was the rightful ruler of Phrygia. When he defeated the Persians, the legend had even more power.

Legendary places

Many places have legends attached to them. A well-known English legend is that of the Lambton Worm. Read the extracts over the next few pages and see if you can piece together the story yourself.

DURHAM GAZETTE

Fierce Beast Ravages Land and Steals Sheep

The people of the small north-eastern hamlet of Lambton live in fear tonight as a <u>fierce and highly poisonous monster has taken</u> <u>control of the countryside there</u> **2** **3** .

Known as a 'worm', the locals describe it as an enormous and terrifying reptile. It has taken sheep and other livestock. Local farmer Ted Penrose said that the creature emerged from a nearby well.

"It must have been there for years to have grown so big. I've lost several lambs and some of my best **ewes**, too."

Dear Father,

It fills me with horror to hear that the worm has caused such devastation and I feel that <u>my wild behaviour as a young man is in some way to blame</u> ④. I had hoped that it would go away when I left Lambton but it seems not. <u>I will return and not rest until the worm is destroyed</u> ⑤!

Your devoted son,
<u>John Lambton</u> ①

Lambton Horror

Three men are <u>reported dead today, and a further five are missing</u> ② from the troubled village of Lambton. <u>Several brave volunteers</u> ① had gone out to challenge the **infamous** Lambton Worm as it coiled around the sides of a local hill.

"We didn't stand a chance," one lucky survivor reported. "<u>We'd cut one piece off it and it would just reattach itself. There's no way we can kill it</u> ②. A brave knight with a charmed life is what we need now, to send this monster back from whence it came!"

Tragedy as Lambton Worm Crisis Deepens

Villagers and farmers of Lambton gathered at church today to remember the lives of several children who were killed by the Lambton Worm last week.

"Action must be taken," said one distraught local. "<u>The monster is taking people now</u> ②."

DURHAM GAZETTE

Dear Sir,

I have been reading with dismay about the frightful creature that is terrorizing Lambton at the moment and I can lay the blame for its existence fairly and squarely at the door of Lord John Lambton, your local squire.

Several years ago, I chanced upon him fishing at the side of the River Wear one Sunday morning. He showed me a creature he had caught and it was a tiny version of the **fiend** that plagues you now.

I told him to throw it back in the river but <u>he threw it in the well instead</u> **4**.

Angry from Rickleton

Advice from local wise woman to John Lambton

1 It is your fault that the worm is here. <u>You have to kill it</u> **5**.

2 Get a blacksmith to stick spearheads on your suit of armour. This will stop the worm from crushing you.

3 Fight the worm in the river. When you cut it in half, the water will wash the other half away before it can heal itself.

4 To lift the curse of the worm, when it is dead you must kill the first living thing that you meet on your way home.

5 If you don't do this, <u>no Lambton will die peacefully for nine **generations**</u> **4**.

Triumph! Lambton Worm is Dead

Local lord kills beast but doesn't join in the celebrations

Dear John,

I'm sorry that I ran out to meet you after you slew the beast. In my joy and pride, I forgot that you had to slay the first living thing you met on the road home. Yet I am glad you spared my life.

I just hope the curse doesn't come true (4).

Your loving father

Lambton Local Guidebook

Some say that you can still make out steps which were cut into the hill by the body of the worm. These were formed as it slept coiled around it (9)!

Why not try and write the complete story of the Lambton Worm? Or find out about a landmark near you that has a legend attached to it.

Legendary planning

By now you should be feeling inspired enough to start creating your own legend. Let's remind ourselves about the features you should think about including in your story and explore some ideas to get you started.

1 Most legendary figures are said to have existed in the real world, so they will start off as real men and women.

My hero or heroine will still have to be impressive. I'll give them a useful skill such as speed, strength or intelligence.

2 There needs to be a villain, threat or problem.

The problem could be an enemy army or a natural disaster that people need to be rescued from.

3 Monsters and strange creatures feature less in legends.

4 There may be unintended consequences of your hero's actions.

If I do include a fearsome creature, perhaps it should be a real animal like a bear or a lion.

They might have to **sacrifice** themselves, or fight an even greater enemy once the first is defeated.

5 There could be a quest or mission to undertake.

I want my story to be exciting. I'll need to put my hero in danger!

It could be based on a local legend from my home town.

6 The story will be set a long time ago, but in a real location.

7 People may claim that gods have helped them in a legend, but gods rarely appear or get too involved.

A god might send my hero a sign at the end of the story, such as thunder or lightning.

8 There may be special objects or weapons used.

Special objects or weapons don't have to be enchanted, but they should be useful!

I want to give my story a memorable ending – even if it's a sad one.

9 Remember: unlike a myth, a legend doesn't usually explain how something came into being.

Now, before you launch into writing your own myth or legend, have a look at some of the ingredients in more depth …

Ingredients Directory
Heroes and heroines ①

Both myths and legends contain heroic characters, and often the line between myth and legend can become blurred. People believed many myths about the legendary Alexander the Great, including that his sister was a mermaid!

Sometimes heroes are super-tough and super-strong, sometimes they are weak but extremely clever. This table shows the characteristics of three heroic figures: Heracles and Atalanta from Greek mythology, and Rostam from Persian legend.

	Heracles	Rostam	Atalanta
Super-strong	✓	✓	✓
Clever and resourceful	✓	✓	✓
Completed impossible tasks/went on quests	✓	✓	✓
Lived for a long time	✓	✓	
Almost invincible in battle	✓	✓	✓
Killed by treachery	✓	✓	

Heracles is tricked into wearing a shirt soaked in the poisonous blood of the Hydra, an evil monster with many heads ③. The blood burns into his skin and he is in so much pain that he decides to die.

Rostam's <u>half-brother kills him</u> 2 by digging a pit filled with poisoned spears and tricking Rostam into falling into it.

Speedy Atalanta will only marry a man who can beat her in a race. One of her suitors slows her down with the help of <u>Aphrodite, the goddess of love</u> 7 .

Some heroes of myth and legend may be physically strong but make mistakes. Or things may go wrong even though they are doing everything right. <u>Rostam kills his own son in battle because he doesn't know him</u> 4 .

Some heroes have weaknesses that they keep secret. The Ancient Greek hero <u>Achilles could only be hurt by wounding a small area around his heel</u> 2 .

Give your hero or heroine a weakness. It makes the story more interesting because there is a chance he or she might fail!

Villains 2

Of course, if you've got an awesome hero or heroine, then you need an awesome villain to make life difficult! Stories, whether they are in myths, legends, novels or films, are often accounts of characters overcoming obstacles and challenges to achieve something. Defeating a villain is the ultimate challenge for our heroes – that's why we need them.

Try to figure out which villain would win in a battle of strength, sneakiness and **malevolence!**

Shaghad

Rostam's jealous half-brother who digs a pit and fills it with poisoned spears so that Rostam will fall into it when he rides by. He succeeds, proving just how **devious** he is!

Strength	6
Sneakiness	8
Malevolence	7

Hera

Heracles's wicked stepmother who drives him insane and makes him kill people. She hates Heracles and is always plotting his death.

Strength	8
Sneakiness	9
Malevolence	8

Mordred

The son of King Arthur (or, in some versions, his nephew). Mordred tries to overthrow Arthur and rule Camelot. Arthur kills him in the end but receives a deadly wound himself.

Strength	6
Sneakiness	7
Malevolence	9

Set

In Egyptian mythology, this god kills Osiris and chops him up so he can't be reborn. For sheer evilness, he can't be beaten!

Strength	7
Sneakiness	5
Malevolence	10

King Minos

King of Crete and creator of the maze that houses a deadly **Minotaur**. Minos demands that seven young men and seven young women are to be fed to the monster every nine years.

Strength	4
Sneakiness	4
Malevolence	9

Invent your own villain

Why not create some villain cards for yourself? Decide on some evil characteristics for your villains and give them a score out of 10. Use a villain card to challenge your hero when you write your own myth or legend!

Monsters and Creatures 3

You don't have to have a monster in your story but, as we've seen from the tale of the Lambton Worm, a scaly beast can make a legend special!

First, decide what your monster is for. Does it guard something? <u>Is it sent by the villain to destroy your hero? Is it threatening a town or village</u> 2 ? How does it attack? Is it poisonous? Does it breathe fire? How does it protect itself? With scaly armour or a thick skin?

Many monsters from ancient cultures are creatures made up of several different animal parts:

Hippocampus
Horse + fish = hippocampus
Probably the strangest creature thought up by the Ancient Greeks!

Gryphon
Lion + eagle = gryphon
A king among mythical beasts!

Manticore
Man + lion = manticore
Comes with rows of razor teeth and a scorpion's tail!

Random monster generator

Pick a number between 1 and 6, or roll a dice. Your monster will have the *head* of a:

1	2	3	4	5	6
lion	bull	dragon	wolf	eagle	snake

Your monster will have the *body* of a:

1	2	3	4	5	6
crocodile	horse	ostrich	giraffe	zebra	orangutan

Your monster will have the *tail* of a:

1	2	3	4	5	6
scorpion	shark	skunk	lizard	fox	rat

Don't forget to think up a brilliant name for your monster that will strike fear into any hero's heart!

Where does it live?

Your monster could be based at sea, like the sea serpents that populate many of the world's mythologies. Or in a dark, underground lake. It could be a forest-and-mountain monster like a Sasquatch. Maybe it lives in a cave like the dreaded one-eyed giant, Cyclops. If it is guarding something, then it might be wise to have it living wherever that something is!

Defeating your monster

In some stories, the hero beats the monster by sheer strength alone, but it's a lot more fun to set up a tricky way to kill a monster. It makes the hero seem clever and makes his or her task harder, too.

The Lernaean Hydra

The Hydra lived in a foul-smelling lake and its body and blood were highly **venomous**. It had many heads and when one was cut off, two more grew in its place (4). One of its heads was immortal (3)(2). Heracles (1) had to defeat this monster (5). He knew he couldn't do it on his own, so he took his nephew, Iolaus (1).

Every time Heracles cut off a head, Iolaus would **scorch** the stump of the neck with a burning torch. This stopped the Hydra from growing more heads.

Finally, only the immortal head remained. Heracles cut it off with a golden sword given to him by the goddess Athena (8).

He took the still-writhing head and buried it deep under a huge stone.

Did you notice any similarities between the Hydra and the Lambton Worm? John Lambton had special armour made and killed the monster in a fast-flowing river so that its body couldn't join together again.

Fatal flaws

Just like your hero or heroine, it can be good to give your monster a weakness. This is a flaw that your hero must somehow discover, but it should be hard to take advantage of. After all, the confrontation must still be a challenge or else the monster poses no threat.

Pick a flaw!

- Gap or crack in its armour – just big enough for a sword to slide in.
- Sunlight – just keep your monster occupied until the sun comes up!
- Sensitivity to a **substance** that wouldn't harm ordinary people – such as salt or sand.

Real monsters

If you are writing a legend, your hero could face huge grizzly bears, crocodiles or sharks. There are plenty of fearsome creatures to choose from if you don't want to make one up.

The legendary **kraken** might just be based on sightings of enormous squid in the Antarctic Ocean. Specimens of this colossal squid have been found, measuring up to 13 metres in length!

Quests ⑤

Quests are long journeys, often to <u>far-off lands</u> ⑥ where <u>strange and dangerous</u> <u>beasts</u> ③ dwell. Quests are great to include in your myths or legends because they give your character a goal and exciting challenges to overcome. Have a browse through the brochure below and choose the right quest for your hero!

Welcome to Hero Quests

We guarantee the toughest challenges and the most distant lands for you to explore!

The Maze of the Minotaur at Knossos

This is our 'short-stay' option for heroes who like an indoor holiday. All you have to do is find the centre of the maze, kill the Minotaur and return home with two princesses.

Optional extra: A ball of twine to unroll behind you so you can find your way out again!

Theseus gave this five stars on Quest Advisor.

The Gruelling Green Knight Grand Tour

Travel all over England, searching for the giant Green Knight. You'll encounter misty marshes, strange castles and a green giant who wants to cut your head off!

"I really found this quest a tough one." – Sir Gawain

The Viking Voyage

Save a quaint village from an evil monster who just hates anyone having fun. Rip its arm off and have the party of a lifetime!
Beowulf gave this quest five stars, adding, "Even though lots of my old friends got eaten, I met new ones who were more interesting!"

Argonaut Adventure

The cruise that has it all! Find a golden fleece which is guarded by a dragon that never sleeps. Before that, you must face six-armed giants and moving cliffs that want to crush your boat.
"I topped up my tan and improved my sword skills on this epic journey." – Jason

If you set a quest as the basis for your myth or legend, make sure you have a good reason for including it. Is it a rescue mission? Is a special object needed to save someone's life? Has the hero or heroine done something wrong that only completing the quest can put right?

Far-off Lands 6

You have to have a setting for your story, but which of these mythical or legendary locations could you travel to today?

1. *Timbuktu*: People in the United Kingdom used to describe this city as a far-off and exotic place at the ends of the Earth.

2. *El Dorado*: When Spain colonized parts of South America they found so much gold among the native tribes that it sparked rumours of a city made entirely of gold.

3. *Atlantis* was said to be an island or continent that sank beneath the sea.

4. In Irish mythology, the land of *Tir Na Nog* is the land of eternal youth. A day in Tir Na Nog is the same as many years in the real world.

5. *Knossos*: **Archaeologists** have never found evidence of the maze where the terrifying Minotaur is said to have lived.

Answers: Timbuktu and Knossos

Why not plan the features of your far-off land by drawing a map? You might include perilous mountains, murky swamps, deadly deserts or stormy jungles. Let your imagination go wild!

Gods 7

Gods can be a great addition to a myth story, and they might even creep into a legend. Your hero could be the child of a god, like Heracles, Perseus or the legendary hero Gilgamesh, who was described as being 'one-third mortal'.

Gods can <u>send heroes on quests</u> ⬤5 , give them <u>enchanted weapons</u> ⬤8 or information, and even step in at the last moment to save them, but beware – having a god involved doesn't always mean you are unstoppable. <u>It might be that the gods in your story don't want your hero to succeed</u> ⬤2 . This is a great way of making life difficult for your main character and creating challenges. You might not want to make enemies of these two ...

Loki

Loki, a god from **Norse** mythology, is often portrayed as a trickster. Sometimes he helps other gods and heroes, other times he insults them and works against them.

Hera

Heracles's stepmother, Hera, drove him so mad that he killed his wife and children.

A Final Twist in the Tale

Anyone reading or listening to a story loves a surprise or shock. What if your hero feels sorry for the monster? What if they become best friends? Perhaps a main character will be killed off before the end, or maybe your myth or legend is written from the villain's point of view. The hero might not sound so wonderful then ...

Why not make it unclear who the hero is at first, or write about a most unlikely hero? He or she could be a coward with an unusual weapon, such as the Spoon of Light!

There are plenty of legends about heroes in mythology who had all kinds of animal sidekicks. Who wouldn't want to ride on Pegasus, the winged horse? If you are going to write a legend, it could be a story about a legendary pet! Your explanation myth could even be about something really silly, for example: "And that's why teenagers are always grumpy."

An unexpected twist in the tale will really entertain your audience.

My Last Word ...

I really love myths and legends. They put us in touch with the past, either by telling us tales about the exploits of people in the past or by telling us how people thought about and understood the world.

Myths and legends will overlap. Myths develop about people who really lived. Sometimes the events of their lives are told and details added.

The real fun is in telling and writing these kinds of stories. All you need is a hero or heroine, a far-off land, a monster or a special weapon and you can set off on new adventures.

So go on! Write a brilliant myth or make up a stunning legend, and who knows? People may still be telling it in a thousand years time!

Glossary

alchemy: an ancient version of chemistry, mostly involving changing one type of metal to another or finding a way to live for ever

archaeologists: people who study the past by examining objects, remains and buildings

colonize: to take over a place and settle in it

devious: sly, tricky, not to be trusted

drastic: severe or extreme

eternal youth: the state of being young for ever

ewes: female sheep

fiend: a monster or villain

generations: stages in a family's timeline, characterized by a group of people born at the same time

immortal: able to live for ever

infamous: well known for doing a bad thing

kraken: a sea monster thought to be like a giant squid or octopus

malevolence: being very evil and cruel

Minotaur: a monster from Greek mythology with a man's body and a bull's head

mortal: an ordinary person who will eventually die

natural phenomenon (plural: **phenomena**): an event that happens in the natural world, e.g. birds migrating, volcanoes erupting, or lightning

Norse: to do with Vikings

sacrifice: to give up something important

scorch: to burn the surface

substance: a material

terrorizes: frightens or threatens

Titan: one of the oldest Greek gods

urban legend: a type of modern myth, which some people insist is true

venomous: poisonous

Index

About the Author

I'm an award-winning children's author. Many of my books are inspired by traditional folk songs and stories, and by myths and legends.

I live on the marshes of Wirral, which is mentioned in the poem *Sir Gawain and the Green Knight* as a misty land full of villains, but it's a nice place really. I enjoy running and playing the mandolin. If I were a mythical hero, I would wear seven-league boots and rescue princesses and kittens in them. If I were a mythical villain, I would wear seven-league boots and kidnap princesses and kittens in them!

Greg Foot, Series Editor

I've loved science ever since the day I took my papier mâché volcano into school. I filled it with far too much baking powder, vinegar and red food colouring, and WHOOSH! I covered the classroom ceiling in red goo. Now I've got the best job in the world: I present TV shows for the BBC, answer kids' science questions on YouTube, and make huge explosions on stage at festivals!

Working on TreeTops inFact has been great fun. There are so many brilliant books, and guess what ... they're all packed full of awesome facts! What's your favourite?